$HIT THEY NEVER TAUGHT YOU IN LAW SCHOOL

$HIT THEY NEVER TAUGHT YOU IN LAW SCHOOL

The Survival Guide to Navigating the Law

JASON S. WEISS, ESQ.

Jason S. Weiss, Esq.
jason@jswlawyer.com
https://www.jswlawyer.com/

$hit They Never Taught You in Law School, Jason S. Weiss, Esq. —1st ed. ISBN 9781955242875

DEDICATION

When I started the process of writing this book, I was given the option to dedicate it to someone. I was not keen on the idea, and I quickly passed on the offer.

Here we are, less than sixty days later, and I now want to dedicate this book to one of the most amazing people I have ever met and loved: My Dad, Bruce Weiss. From when I started this book until the time I finished the first draft, my Dad had a cardiac event on an airplane, was hospitalized in the ICU in Atlanta, Georgia (even though he lived in Florida) and passed away. Now I can dedicate this book to a person who meant the world to me. Dad knew I was writing this book and he loved to read, so what an ideal tribute to an amazing dad, grandpa and husband!

My Dad is a man who lived his life. He loved everything he did. From going to my baseball games as a kid, to kickball as an adult, to lacrosse and dance for his grandkids and yelling at the TV when his team was losing, Grampie, as my daughter Madison calls him, loved being present and living in the moment. Dad was the guy who wanted to do it all and tried his best to do that! I have to admit, growing up, he was not a softie in any respect. But he was never mean or rude, just tough.

I found out from my mom after my Dad passed away that he loved being a grandfather so he could spoil "his amazing grandkids." No spend was too much and no ask was too big. I always remember when I was growing up, Dad managed to provide for our family and always was there to support us. He was so proud of his three boys, his two daughters-in-law, his five grandkids, and my mom (his soulmate).

Dad got softer as time went on and was the "best grandpa ever". Let me tell you, Dad left his mark. When my Dad passed away, one of my best friends, David Block, who wrote the foreword, texted me and told me that he was sitting at his desk with tears rolling down his face, as it was so rare in life to meet such a wonderful, caring person like my Dad.

I was so lucky to get to say that I got to work with my Dad two days a week. He would come to the office, set up his spot, play music and chit chat around the office. He had a cheese stick, pretzels, M&Ms and a bottle of water each day for lunch, coupled with bad jokes and football pools. My dad lived his life to the fullest, and nothing got in his way.

My Dad was and still is an amazing man.

Everyone who knew him was lucky to just have the chance to meet him. I miss him, love him, and know he is watching over me now like I am part of his favorite TV show. I love you, Dad. Thank you for helping me become the man, husband, father, and person I am. I am forever grateful for all you did, your unwavering support and love, and for the example you set for the rest of us. You are the inspiration for finishing this book, and I am using you as my motivation. To Bruce, with Love!!

CONTENTS

.

Foreword

by David J. Block, Esq.

A quick summary of my background explains how I was eventually introduced to Jason. I am a 1992 graduate of the University of Miami Law School. Following law school, I practiced as an attorney for five years before I found my calling as a legal recruiter. What is a legal recruiter? I help my clients (law firms and corporations) find attorneys for specific opportunities they may have at their organization.

Nearly twenty years ago, Jason contacted me regarding the possibility of changing law firms. He tried to convince me that with one year of experience under his belt, he should be considered for a 2-5 year position. Who would have known at the time that I was about to meet someone who has become one of my closest friends, a business partner, confidant and sounding board.

I learned over the years that Jason was a very good baseball player. In baseball terms, he would be considered a five-tool prospect – basically, he was good at everything. Well, he didn't make it to the major leagues. However, fortunately for me and many others – **he is a five-tool friend.**

Jason is very smart and a good teacher; supremely organized; loyal, reliable and trustworthy; funny; and he is one of the kindest and most giving individuals you could ever meet.

As a legal recruiter, I have met many highly intelligent individuals. Many of the candidates have graduated from top twenty law schools and are working at the best firms in the country. However, many of these attorneys are only book-smart. Meanwhile, Jason has more than pure intelligence. He has EQ - emotional quotient. He is a relationship-builder and the empathy he shows to colleagues and friends helps him to relate with almost everybody. He is always available to provide sage advice on how to handle different business and personal situations.

Jason is the most organized person I have ever met. As a business partner – we owned a business and a building together – we were like the "odd couple". I am an ADD-addled, forgetful and disorganized adult, while he is mindful, supremely organized and always has tasks done on time or ahead of time. Frequently, I would ask him to remind me of this function or that deadline, and without fail, he would remember to update me on that day.

Jason is reliable, loyal and trustworthy. You can ask Jason for anything – whether it's to drive you to the airport, pick up your child from an event, or edit your child's essay. He will handle whatever is needed, without asking questions, and will make sure it is completed on time. He prides himself on doing his best the first time so that he does not need to do it again.

Jason has always been funny. He will bust your chops with one-liners and crack everyone up. He can ease the tension in a room with a quick zinger said at the appropriate time – (timing is critical in making people laugh).

What I have come to appreciate most about Jason is the kindness of his heart. When my father was sick and I had to travel to Buffalo for extended periods, Jason would call and text me to express his concern and to offer help to my family with whatever may be needed. A one-of-a-kind friend who is there for you in good times and bad. **You can't put a price on that**!

INTRODUCTION

How do I know what I don't know? Think about that for a moment. Re-read it to make sure you understand the question. How do I know what I don't know? That's a great ask (even if I do say so myself).

That is the question that I would like to help you address. I will not answer the question for you; that is not the reason behind this book. This is not the "book of answers", but rather the book of reflection and the book to help guide you. It will help you on your way, but it will not show you the way. That is on you!

What I can assure you is that this book will help you learn some of the shit they did not teach you in law school. Not because you went to a bad school or because you did not pay attention in class (or did not get a good grade), but because of the real life "stuff" that is not part of any curriculum. This book covers the shit you never thought about, like the business side or the personal aspects of the law. Look at this as a guide on how to navigate the profession. Think of me as the little person sitting on your shoulder who you ask questions to. In the end, you answer your own questions, but I am your sounding board.

You went to law school with the idea that you would graduate knowing everything, ready to tackle cases, clients and everything else you need to have a successful career. What you do not know, you will learn on the job, and you will develop skills over the course of your career. But where do you go to learn? Who can you lean on for help? How do you know if you are ready?

Your hope is that law school taught you what you need to know to go out and crush it, but what if you did not get to take all of the classes you wanted during your three years? I assure you, no matter how amazing of a student you were and no matter how great your internships were, you will not be 100% ready for this journey (even today, twenty-three years in, I am still learning on a daily basis). But that is a good thing. There are a ton of things you do not learn in school, but that you "get to" learn on the fly, and (hopefully) you have a mentor or an advisor to help you on your way. Hence the reason for this book: to help you see some of the $hit you never learned in law school.

For me, it all began in the winter of 1984 when I was eight years old. I remember riding in the back of my Poppi's Chevy station wagon, in the way, way back facing backwards (the third row that was in the trunk). We pulled up to the tennis club that my uncle was a member of. I got out of the car, and there it was: my cousin's Jaguar. It was one of the coolest cars I had ever seen up close and personal. I turned to my mom and asked her, "Mom, what does Cousin Bruce do for a job?" I knew my Uncle Steve was a surgeon, and that was why he was driving a Mercedes and could have us as guests at the club, but I did not know what Bruce did. My mom told me he was a lawyer. That's all I needed to hear: become a lawyer and drive a nice car. Done.

In that single moment, becoming an attorney replaced my less realistic prior job choice of being a fire truck (yes, you read that correctly, being a fire truck, not a firefighter). My goals were in place and my destiny was determined.

The most ironic part of this is that when I saw Bruce many years later (when I was already in practice for more than eighteen years), I found out for the first time that the Jaguar was part of a barter with a client who could not pay a bill, and it was falling apart. It looked good on the outside but was not mechanically sound. Imagine if I had asked him about the car and how he got it when I was younger? I may have gone the medical route (doubt it, as I would need to tackle my dislike for blood, hospitals, and hard science classes) or done anything else. Maybe that single question would have changed my entire career. I cannot, will not, and do not live my life on "what if's," but it is still okay to ponder that for a moment. I guess doing research is a necessity.

I had my plan, and I was on my way. I would work hard in high school to go to a good college, work hard in college to go to law school, take the bar, get a license, and then be on the path to success, financial freedom, and my nice car. My road map was set, and I was more than ready (or so I thought). I did well in high school and went to the University of Florida (GO GATORS). I met my wife there as well (added bonus for me). I got accepted to a few law schools and decided that I would go to law school in a state and city where I eventually wanted to live. I wanted to be in South Florida, so the University of Miami (UM) is where I went.

I went to UM wanting to be the next Jerry Maguire and/or the attorney for the "mob". That bubble popped pretty quickly, and I went on to be an intern for the Department of Justice Executive Office of Immigration Review for two summers. I really enjoyed Immigration Law, but I was not able to be placed in a full-time role in South Florida, and I would have had to be willing to relocate to Brooklyn, Louisiana, Texas, or one or two other states. I did not want to relocate from Florida, so my career in Immigration Law was over before it began.

I studied for the Florida Bar like it was a full-time job and then some. Six days a week of studying. I went to Bar prep classes on campus during the week (8am-3pm) and then came home to study more. Wake up, go to campus. Attend classes and do practice questions in between. Go home, have dinner with my wife, and back to the books until I could not keep my eyes open any longer. What did I do??

Saturdays were not much better. I would wake up a little later and study for the day. Date night with my wife and then bed. Sunday would be for time with my wife (shopping, lunch, and relaxing). We would be home after lunch at the mall food court of the Big Cheese in Miami, prepare for the rest of the week, and I would study here and there. I did this all of June and all of July. What a grind.

I did it!!! I passed the bar on my first go around, and I was ready to make millions and millions of dollars! Unlike now, there was no Uniform Bar Exam, so I only took Florida, but I did well enough that I was able to waive into the District of Columbia a few years later. Keep in mind that I left a lot of the middle steps out of this story, and I will sprinkle them in throughout this book. But this book is not about me. The bottom line was that law school was not all it was made out to be, and despite getting a great education, I had no clue what was in store for me. I really learned so much about the law once I was out of the classroom and in the "real world" (not the courtroom, as I spent most days behind my desk). That is the motive behind writing this book – to give an insight into real life law and to help you each step of the way.

You may be asking, especially if you did not go to law school, "What kinds of problems could he have armed with a law degree and "only" $88,000+ in debt?"

We all have problems, and many of them are common for newbie attorneys (like I was). Do I consolidate my loans? Do I take the job that would help me make money fast or the job where I can see myself in the long run? What if the area of law I thought I wanted to do was not really for me? What if I regret taking the job I took? I have a hearing coming up, and I have no clue what I am doing. Who can I ask for help? How do I enter my time so the bills get paid? How do I know how to bill and what to bill? Can I leave before my boss leaves, or do I need to stay and be the last one here every night? Can I leave a bit earlier on a Friday? What if I am not in the office before my boss? What if I receive an email late at night, and I don't want to respond? What if I have a missed call from the office and do not know who to call back?

These problems (and so many more) are all normal, and it is not your fault for not knowing the answer (or if there is an answer) because you were never taught any of this. This is where law school fails.

I admit that professors and school can only teach you so much. Law School teaches you how to follow, interpret, and enforce the law. There is so much stuff they do not get to teach you in the classroom. There should be a mandatory externship or an additional semester to prepare you for real life as an attorney. The business of law. The practice of law. The "how to be a good attorney" class. The "this is what it truly is like" course. Learning does not end when you leave school or have your degree. Learning is a process that will continue way beyond the classroom. You need to be willing to keep learning and keep going. That is why we practice!

I am fortunate (and unfortunate) enough to say I think I have seen it all, and I have learned from it (and from some of the best of the best). I am not saying that I have not learned from my mistakes (as I 100% have), but rather that I have grown from all of my experiences. I have been through plenty and want to help others as they are trying to navigate through this profession. I am more like your personal tour guide. I want to show you the things you might want to check out while on the tour, but you are free to follow, leave, or add comments at any time. I just want to be the person for you who I wish I had when I was getting out of school. I had some amazing people help me (thank you Judge Lane for believing in me while I was in law school), and I want to pay it forward (great movie by the way)!

There is so much we need to learn while we are on the job, and these days, with remote work and the ever-changing landscape of the practice of law, this all gets lost. Recent graduates have lofty self-expectations that they can run a case from start to finish and that they "got this". The confidence they exude is honorable and respected, but the truth is, everyone can use a mentor (or a sounding board). I have been very lucky that I have had that most of my professional life (thank you all). I go into more detail about this in the chapter called "Form Your Own Board", but it is just like it sounds.

As someone who has taught various topics of law (Sports Law and Business Law) on the law school, graduate school, and college levels, I wanted to help manage expectations and give a glimmer into the real practice of law, so I am writing this book of tips, lessons, and strategies. I want to educate YOU on $hit They Never Taught You in Law School.

There are so many people I would love to mention and thank on an individual basis, but that list alone would make this Book 500+ pages. I do want to give a shout-out to few people: my wife, Tova; my kids, Logan and Madison; my parents, Bruce and Rose; my grandparents; my brothers Nate and Greg; Uncle Steve and Aunt Estelle; Rina Wolfe; Michael Hofstetter; John Bradley; Josh "Uncle Doodie" Gordon; Uncle Michael Chef Jacobs; Alan Fertel; Mike Golfcart; Judi Hedge; Lee Hofstetter; Joel Rothman; Uncle Milic; Joe Bogart; Max Karyo; Gus Renny; Mitch Ortega; Judge Lane; Auntie Hope; Steve, Marc and Jake Nudelberg; "Coach Gabe" Keding; Randy Ostrow; Pat, Mike and Brian (you know who you are); Sideny and Louis; Mina "iMovers";

Martha Alexander; Sharon Ve; Greg Sconzo; Stefan John; Shameka Cuellar; Stephen Rodriguez; Jeremy Horelick; and the author of the Foreword, David Block. These people (as well as many others) have been on my personal Advisory Board (which I will explain later on in the book... I give credit to Steve Nudelberg for introducing me to this idea). They are my brain trust and support group. Without them all, I do not know where I would be!

Like the Beatles say, "I get by with a little help from my friends." Let me tell you, I am here to be your friend (and hopefully help you do more than just get by). I want you to have health, wealth, happiness, and success (however you decide to define these four things). What all of that looks like will be unique to you. Remember (in addition to what I cover in Chapter 6), you need to be able to look yourself in the mirror and be content (with the goal being for you to be happy with what you see).

Let's do this thing (I picture Linguini from the movie Ratatouille)!

CHAPTER 1

It is Called the Practice of Law for a Reason

Let's start with the basic concept that law is not like science or math where things are black and white and there are right and wrong answers. Law is the gray area. It is called the practice of law (like the practice of medicine) for a reason. Why?? There is right, wrong, and gray. What do I mean? Read on.

You can make the same arguments (written or oral) in front of a judge or jury, and you can either win or lose. You can score a huge win, and your client could not see the win the same way. You can get a partial ruling in your favor and a partial ruling against you. Would the outcome be different if you were in front of another judge? Law is NOT black and white.

A great example is that you can apply for a trademark with the United States Patent and Trademark Office, and you can tell your client that he or she has a chance to get the registration, but there is also a chance it can be denied. You, the client, and the world will not know until you submit the application and go through the review process. What is the end result? We need to wait and see what the examiner determines. It is a waiting game (like life).

This makes law very frustrating! You think you have a fantastic case, a great client, all the support you need, the right judge . . . the list goes on and on. However, you lose the case, your client is not happy with you, you are doing your own filing at 2AM, your bills remain unpaid, a judge rules against you without any reason or you are just stuck. WTF???

This is all typical for an attorney beginning his or her career (or even for a seasoned attorney). Does it suck? Sure does. Will it upset you, bug you and keep you up at night? Yep, even now, twenty-three years in, I cannot say things like the above do not happen and do not get to me. Heck, I think if it did not get to me, then it may mean that I did not care and that maybe it is time to find something else to do.

These obstacles do not go away, and they can even accumulate over the years if you cannot recognize them and tackle them head on when you start off. You want to make sure you begin on the right foot. That first step is of utmost importance. It is easier to learn the correct things from the start instead of needing to unlearn and re-learn.

I remember when my son, Logan, was just getting into lacrosse, and we took him to a trainer to work on his footwork and speed. His first step out of the box was slow. Why? He was doing a back step and then going forward. Once he trained himself to take the first step forward, wow, he was off and running, and what a difference it made. Now, he takes the first step quickly and without needing to think about it.

Heck, he gets faster and faster on a daily basis ((jumping rope helps too). You need to make sure your first step is forward, not backward! Start with your best foot forward.

The question many of us have asked ourselves is: what don't I know? That is the ten-billion-dollar question. We can delve deep into how problems affect the lives of attorneys and the emotions that come with them (frustration, confusion, stress, etc.), but first and foremost, remember it is the practice of law. The goal of this chapter (and the book as a whole) is to show you that you need to understand the situations you will need to handle and be prepared for them.

Most often, problems are not avoidable, but if you can anticipate them, you will be much happier. Something as simple as keeping in mind that it is the practice of law will help you face this head on (and it will not hurt to have me as your personal tour guide through the rough terrain).

Law is not one size fits all, and you need to be able to adjust how you look at situations and sometimes think outside of the box. That is the part of the law I enjoy: getting to use the creative side of my brain. When you have a guide with you, your experience will be so much more enjoyable and effective.

One of the things I loved doing when I was at Big Law (and even when I started my own practice) was helping with the internship program and molding future (or rookie) attorneys.

When we would work on a pleading or a case, I would get the "Well, we have the law on our side, so we cannot lose" or the "We can win if . . . But we would lose if. . .". This is such a law school habit that needs to be overcome (or nipped in the bud before it starts).

Just because a case says the court should rule in a certain way, that does not mean it is automatic (the same goes when you are on the less fortunate side of the case law). Having the law on your side does not mean you win. It helps you bolster your argument, but do not count on that for the win. I have had cases where there was no way I could lose (and yes, you can guess it, I lost), and I have made arguments that were such a stretch but resulted in a win.

Also, in your writing, you do not want to tell the Court (or someone else), "We win if ABC happens, but we lose if XYZ happens." That might be fine and dandy (and possibly even expected) when you sit with a client or write a paper in school, but it will not be okay in a demand letter, a pleading, or something else. You have to advocate for your client and believe in the position you take. Is it right? Maybe, but that is why it is the practice of law (and not an exact science). You cannot fake it until you make it, but you can try various arguments and angles and see what works. Give it the ole college try.

The same applies to medicine. While I was in the process of writing this book, my father went through a significant medical issue (his heart stopped when he was on an airplane flying back to the US from visiting my brother in Germany). He was rushed to Grady Memorial Hospital in Atlanta (where he and my mother had a layover), and they tried it all with him. Treatments, breathing tubes, pacemaker, defibrillator, mixtures of meds prayer . . . All with the goal in mind of allowing him to be discharged and go home to live his life. But there was never a clear-cut answer of, "If we do X, then Y will happen." They tried and tried and tried and tried. That is the same in the practice of law.

How do you get to Carnegie Hall? Practice, Practice, Practice.

CHAPTER 2

You are Only as Good as Your Book of Business.

For those readers who do not know the term "book of business", it is your client base, your client list, or your customers (however you define that). It is the following of clients that you have (people who would "go with you" if you moved firms or started your own business).

You could be the best litigator or transactional attorney to ever walk into a courtroom or a conference room, but if you do not have clients to service, then what good is having all of that skill? David Block instilled this philosophy in me when I was a rookie attorney. I saw a posting on a job board for an attorney position (it was for a 2-5 year attorney, and I had just started my second year of practice). David was kind and generous with his time, and he gave me the advice that I have used for the past 20+ years: go out and get clients. Service your clients and take good care of them. Repeat business will make you marketable and will help you in the long run, with either starting your own practice or making partner at a law firm.

Well, I listened to David, and here I sit with my own law firm, an amazing group of fantastic clients and the freedom to follow the career path of my choosing. Don't be fooled--I will admit it was not always like that. But starting with my first client to the clients I have today, you need to make sure you have enough of a book of business to make you valuable and marketable.

Before you know it, these clients become more than clients and are a part of your life and family (hence why my kids have "Uncle Milic", who is an amazing man who I am proud to call "My Brotha"). This man would do anything to make sure I am better than okay and that I am safe, taken care of and never in harm's way.

When I first opened Weiss Law Group, P.A., my primary area of practice was door law: I would take any case that came in the door. Now twelve years later as the managing partner of my own firm and more than twenty-three years in practice, I can be more selective and work with clients I choose. This was all possible based on the advice of David, and for that I thank him.

So, my advice for you: go develop a client list and your own book of business. "But how, Jason, how do I do that?" I would begin by making a simple list or chart of people you want to target. It can be industries, actual people, geographic areas, or anything that works for you. It is okay if your book starts with family, friends, and neighbors. Sometimes, they are more willing to give you the opportunity to help them out. I have included a chart at the end of this chapter for you to use as a guide (and to tweak so it works well for you).

What else can you do? Keep reading the next few chapters in this book, make sure you do things that make you happy when you are not "at work" and keep your eye on the prize – what you define as being successful (which will vary from person to person and there is no right or wrong answer).

Get out there, do things you like, and develop a killer elevator pitch. Be prepared for the question, "What do you do for a living?" Don't just say, "I'm an attorney." Make it more interesting and specific.

I told people what I did by asking them, "Have you ever seen the movie *Pulp Fiction*? Well, I am like The Wolf, I fix things." I also tried saying I was like Olivia Pope from the television show *Scandal* or that I was Ray Donovan. People got it: they saw me as a fixer. I then tried another route. I told people I was Kevlar. I was a bulletproof vest. I cannot prevent people from being shot, but I could protect them from the bullet causing serious harm. These all worked as ice breakers and turned into conversations.

You need to find your own comfort zone and go there. Break the ice however you think it works for you. Try it out. Practice it. See what flows. If it is forced, people will know it, and it will not work!

Potential Clients

Client Name (or Business Name)	Contact Information	Next Steps	Notes

CHAPTER 3

It Will Be Personal

I cannot stress this enough to you – IT WILL BE PERSONAL. The law, clients and cases will all be personal. If you can find a way to separate yourself and make it not personal (and still have passion in what you do), please share with the rest of us. I have been trying to figure it out to no avail.

We can try to remove the emotion and the personal feelings from a case, a client, an opposing counsel, a judge, a *pro se* party (meaning someone who does not have an attorney), or various other people, but let me tell ya, it ain't gonna happen. It will be personal.

You will take it personally if you lose an argument you think you should win. You will take it personally when a client decides not to hire you (or to bring on another attorney to assist you or replace you). You will take it personally when an opposing counsel writes an email or a pleading that you think is just wrong (or not well written). You will take it personally when the court denies a motion like an unopposed motion for extension of time or when you cannot appear at a hearing virtually instead of in person. You will take it personally when someone says something that just boils your blood.

You will take it personally when an opposing counsel says something about a client you truly care about. Trust me, it will be personal, and you will take it personally.

We take it personally because we take it seriously and we care. When we have such thick skin or don't care, we need to do a self-reflection.

If you ask yourself, "Why don't I care anymore?", the answer will be very telling as to where your head is at. Is it that you are now a seasoned attorney and you know better? Is it that you are callous and expect people to be difficult and crappy? Is it that nothing really surprises you anymore? I cannot answer that for you. I know for me it is still personal (and I am just never shocked by what people say or do). I prepare for the worst and hope for the best.

I know this. As I sit here and write this chapter (on a plane from Florida to New Jersey to attend a lacrosse prospect camp with my son), I still take it personally. I have a client who gets demand letters and lawsuits for alleged violations of the telephone consumer protection act (TCPA). When this client gets sued, the client is not overwhelmed with joy, but at the same time, as the owner of the business, he does not take it personally. But I do.

I get angry when this client gets sued and it is the wrong company, there is no proof for the lawsuit, they name the client representative in his personal capacity, there is no basis for the lawsuit or it is just not proper. It pisses me off, and it is apparent in my telephone conversations, emails, motion practice and communications. I get pissed off (often more than the client does). It shows me that I care and that it is personal (or that I at least care a great deal about the person I am representing). It will happen to you too, I promise (and if it does not, then maybe you should consider yourself lucky or reach out to me directly and let me know how you do it).

The trick? Try not to take it soooooo personally that it takes over your head, distracts you, pisses you off so all you can do is dwell on it, upsets you, or just ruins your mood, trip, or day. I know I often need to be reminded of this, and all I hear in my head is my wife singing like Elsa from Frozen – "Let It Go." So I try to listen to Tova's advice, and sometimes, it actually works.

CHAPTER 4

It is OK to Say, "I Do Not Know"

One of the people I find myself leaning on of late is Martha Alexander. She is an Energy Healer and F.I.X. Code Practitioner (and a J.D.). I recommend you look her up and see if she is willing to work with you. What a golden ticket!

When I told Martha in one of our sessions that I was writing this book, she told me that she wished someone would tell newer attorneys (as well as any professional) that it is okay to say, "I don't know."

I know I do that all the time, but it took practice for me to get it down and to say it in my own way. I'll say, "You know what, great question, and I am not sure." I then follow it by saying, "Let me look it up," "Let me get back to you," or even "Let me ask a buddy who might know." That allows me to do some research and look into it.

Yes, people hire attorneys to get answers and get help, but at the same time, we do not know everything. One of the skills we need to make sure clients know we have is that we are good at researching things and we will track down the answer and offer some guidance (and maybe even a solution).

You will not lose a client if you do not know something on the spot (unless you have been asked about it and just failed to do the prior research).

We are humans, we are not AI, and we are not ChatGPT. We are expected to find the answer and give recommendations and options. We can admit we do not know things and let the person know that we would be happy to find out. This is acceptable and a good way to practice (and if it does not work for your client or potential client, then maybe you should consider if you even want said client).

I would recommend developing a "follow up" sheet. What do I mean? See below for a sample.

Date of meeting	Client	Question to Research and findings	Promised Date (or target date)	Completed Date

One additional point that I want to get across is that when you get the answer you want to hear, just stop there and move on. Huh? What does that mean?

Think about this: when you were a kid and wanted to, let's say, go to a party, but you were not sure what your parents would say, you would try to convince them that going to the party was a good thing for them to allow you to do or that you have their permission.

The conversation would go something like this: "Hey Dad, Steve is having a party Saturday night, and I would like to go. Steve's parents will be home, there is no drinking at his house and he only lives twenty minutes away. All of my lacrosse buddies will be there, and we all just want to hang out. I will not be home terribly late and I would love to go. Can I go if I am home before midnight?"

As a parent, my response would be, "What does your Sunday look like? Have you finished all of your school work yet?" My son's response is more often than not that he has lacrosse practice at 9:30AM on Sunday, he has finished all of his homework, and he is getting ahead and studying for a test at the end of the week. My response to that is, "Of course, I know Steve's mom and dad, and I am good with that. Be safe and text me when you get there and when you are on your way home." That is where the conversation should end with my son saying, "Thanks, dad, love ya."

But more often than not, he keeps going. "Ethan will be there as well and so will Mike, Chris and Dan. We all want to watch the college football game and play some fiddle stick lacrosse in the yard. We also want to try this new pizza place and will Uber Eats it to Steve's house." My son will go on and on.

I have already agreed to his "ask," he is not asking for anything more, but he keeps giving more and more information. Why? I am not sure. This is in no way unique to my son or me. I think, as people, we just give more and more. There is nothing he can say to me where I can give him more than he asked for. His ask was to go to the party and be home by midnight. I gave him 100% of what he asked for. So why keep going? I know it took me a while to learn that, but now, I use that in all I do. I ask, I get the answer I want, and I move on and talk about something different.

The same applies in the legal world. When you get what you want, shut up and move on. You do not need to go on and on. Take it, zip your mouth, paper it, and be on your way. You only create issues when you offer more (especially when it is not asked). I am not saying to ever lie. Never lie to the Court, but keep your mouth shut. You got what you wanted, so move on.

No good will ever come of saying too much. So ask, get it, and then say thank you. Thanks for buying this book and reading (and enjoying). Done!

CHAPTER 5

Run (Quickly) From the Client Who Says it is Not About the Money

I have heard it countless times from clients (actual and potential) in my more than twenty-three years of being an attorney: "It is not about the money; it is about the principle." My response to any attorney who hears that from a client (or a potential client) is to run away from that potential case because, I promise you, it will become about the money. However, sometimes you may still decide to take them on as a client, but you need to make sure to have a plan in place as to how you should proceed.

When you have a client who is fired up and wants "revenge" or to prove a point, that desire dies down quickly when the bills begin to mount up. It is all about the spend. When I have these clients that insist they want to fight, fight, fight and money is not an issue, I ask for a larger retainer up front, plus expenses. Instead of the typical amount, I will ask for more. Why? So when he or she wants to dump the case or has a change of heart, I am not left with a huge bill that needs to be paid and a client who says I spent all of this money for what.

If you get the retainer up front, when the client is excited and wants to fight, then it will not bother the client as much (and will not hurt your practice) because you have already been paid for the work. You are prepared for the eventual frustration or exhaustion of the client and you can stay ahead of the potential of a massive unpaid bill.

Another reason for this is that litigation is often long, expensive, stressful and not an efficient use of time. I have been an attorney on the Plaintiff's side and the Defendant's side, and I have been both a Plaintiff and a Defendant. I can tell you, in all four scenarios, I would want the resolution as fast as I could get it (and I was even willing to compromise a bit to have closure).

For me, the principle behind any case is to get the client the best result I can with the least spend by the client as possible. But that is counter-intuitive to how law firms work. Think about the economics of it. If you can resolve a case with a few phone calls and little to no pleadings (or reach a quick settlement), it is the best for the client. The client will pay for your time very happily and make the settlement payments.

Now think about what a law firm wants. Get a large retainer. Bill the file. Draft pleadings and file them with the Court. After motion practice has begun, then you take depositions and send out discovery. Then you are compelled by the Court to attend mediation, and you do so. I am pretty sure that more than 75% of all cases never go to trial, and a large percentage of cases settle at mediation. So instead of spending a ton of time and money, why not go to mediation in the beginning? I love that concept so much that I got certified as a mediator during COVID, and I have been fortunate enough to be able to conduct mediations (and be part of them as an attorney).

One of the things that I recommend to the attorneys I work with is to make sure their clients are aware of what mediation is, that is it available, and that it is not the same as arbitration. I have had many clients who initially refused to go to mediation because they did not know what it was. There was a lot of confusion between arbitration and mediation.

For those of you reading this, the quick summary is that ARBITRATION is binding, and when the arbitrator (or the panel of arbitrators) makes a decision, it is final (as if a court, judge, or a jury made a determination in a trial). MEDIATION, on the other hand, is voluntary and non-binding. So, if at the end you don't want to settle or do not like the "final offers," you can say no thanks and then go to Court. It is a great chance to tell your side of the story, hear the positives and the weaknesses, and see if you can get it resolved. If not, no harm, no foul (as it is completely confidential).

Getting back on the topic of this chapter, I do need to admit that I have one client who is the exception to the norm, and he will tell me that it is not about the money because he needs to teach the other side a lesson. I learned that this client is a man of his word, and there are times he has spent money needlessly because he wanted to teach someone a lesson. This is also a man who is one of the most generous people I know. When he gets the bills, he does not flinch and pays it with a smile (when he felt we were able to teach the lesson he hoped for). For him, it was truly about proving the point, and it was not about the money. But please know this is not what should ever be expected, as he is an anomaly (and a great person and friend).

How do you decide if you want to work with this client who claims it is not about the money (or any potential client)? Follow your gut and listen to your brain. Is the potential for money worth the need to work with a client who you do not particularly care for or for you to work on a matter you do not like? When you are (or were) an associate or when you first started out, you may not have had the freedom (or the authority) to decide which cases and clients you took. But as you build yourself, your book of business, your proactive and your confidence, you get that decision-making power. Use it wisely, as with great power comes great responsibility. I am sure you are saying to yourself right now, "Which clients should I take?" I would tell you to run from the ones who say it is not about the money and give others a chance to see if you mesh well. But in the end, it is your call and you need to do what feels right.

CHAPTER 6

What Would Your Mother, Rabbi or Priest Say?

This is a huge one for me, and I am writing this while on a plane flying home from Richmond, Virginia with Logan. When you make a decision and you are not sure if it is the right one or how you feel about it, ask yourself, "What would my mom say?" or in my case "What would Rabbi Kaplan say?" I like to do what I think is the right thing. Is it always correct? No way, but if it will allow me to sleep at night and not be embarrassed to tell my wife, my kids, my mom, or my Rabbi, then it works for me.

There are so many examples of this, but I can tell you about one instance where I had an employee at the firm, and this employee was there less than the probationary ninety-day period but was just not cutting it. I wanted to let this person go, but this person had a personal matter going on, and I did not want to add insult to injury. So not only did I wait for the personal matter to be resolved, but I also gave this person the option to resign, and I offered severance (despite this person not being entitled to it). Why did I do that? I did it because I felt it was the right thing for me to do and it allowed me to feel less guilty (yes, I felt guilty for letting someone go who did not do the job they were hired for and created more work, cost and aggravation for me). Was this the "best" decision? Not sure. But was it the one that I felt was right? Yes.

This also applies to the timing of when I tell people things. I know I hate it when I get an email at 7pm on a Friday and it requires a response or takes away from my weekend. Unless it is very time sensitive, I will not send emails to clients on Fridays that might ruin their weekend (and I will not send a client a bill on a Friday either; I will hold it until Monday). Why do I do this when people and clients do not show me the same respect? Because that is what my mother and Rabbi would say was nice of me to do.

I want to live my life trying to be a mensch (a good person). I like giving and helping. I feel when I carry on my life like that, I am being the best version of myself that I can be. It may be something small, or it may not be the best thing, but it makes me feel right. There is so much about the profession of law that does not make me feel warm and fuzzy, but these things do help me make it through the day. The law is so confrontational, why not try to make it better?

In order to try to give back, some people live their lives wanting to do one good thing per day. Others push it and do two good things for others each day. Some people volunteer in a soup kitchen or go to church on a Sunday. I used to give out two scratch-off lottery tickets each day and tape a quarter to each one. I would walk up to two random people, hand them the scratch off, and say, "I guarantee you cannot lose." People would say, "Huh, what do you mean?" I told them even if the ticket was not a winner, they were ahead by the quarter attached to it. Most of the time, I would get a chuckle or a "thank you." To me, that response made it all worth it.

A few movies have used the Mark Twain quote that "you are never wrong for doing the right thing." Remember that and do what feels right to you and allows you to feel good. There is no right or wrong answer. And if you are not sure, then think to yourself, what would your Rabbi, Priest or Mother say?

CHAPTER 7

Know Your Audience

I pride myself when people say, "Wait, you are an attorney?" or "You are not a dirtbag attorney." I like when people do not see me coming. I like to talk to people like they are people, not just clients. Let's talk about lacrosse, sports, TV shows, movies, kids… Most of the time, I wear a Vineyard Vines or Longpole Life T-shirt, a pair of shorts, no show black socks, and funky/loud sneakers. Could I wear that to court or on a Zoom hearing? NO!!! NEVER. I wear a white shirt, a red or a blue tie and a black sports jacket (and black suit pants). Why? I know my audience. I do not think any judge would be pleased with my preferred informal attire.

When I have a new client meeting or a client meeting, at a minimum, I wear at least a long-sleeved collared shirt, slacks and modest footwear. When I get to know the client (and it is appropriate), I can dress down and censor my language a bit less. But you need to know your audience.

If you draft a pleading, the first thing you should do is check the local rules and contact the Judicial Assistant (JA) so that you can abide by the judge's procedures. Follow that precisely.

Judges will not tolerate ignorance when a little prep work is all that was needed. Do the same with everything.

Heck, we do that when we travel. Does the airline have screens to watch movies, or should I download something to my phone? Does the airline have headphone jacks, or do I need to charge my wireless ones? Which ones do not have chargers in the seats? You can say that about anything. You must plan ahead. I always plan for the worst and hope for the best (that might not be the best way to live life, but you get the point). I cover this in greater detail in Chapter 12 – PPP.

I know when I prepare a statement for certain mediators, they like to be entertained and enjoy my writing style. One mediator I have used and will continue to use is Steve Jaffe. I like to have him mediate cases because he gets it. He sees the end game and tries to get everyone there. I know when he reads these statements on a daily basis, it is the same ole, boring information each time. Party names, positions, demands, pleadings… I, on the other hand, tell a story. I use the first five to six sentences to grab the reader and to make him want to find out more. Again, it is all about knowing your audience.

On the contrary, I had a settlement conference with a Federal Magistrate Judge in Texas, and I can assure you the statement provided to him was the complete opposite of the one I would send to Jaffe. It was just the facts and advocating for my client and being as conservative and professional as possible.

I know attorneys who love to talk about who they are, where they went to school, how long they have been at the firm, what they practice, and other introductory things. However, many clients don't care, and they do their own research before they walk in the door or take a meeting. Clients do not want to pay to hear how great you are. They want to pay for you to listen to them and help them, not that you have been at this for twenty-five years and you went to an Ivy School. The common icebreaker speech would not work on all clients, and you need to make clients feel special and get to know you. Do your research and know your audience.

I was fortunate enough to work at a firm where we had an amazing Culinary Director (per my kids, Uncle Michael Chef), and he and I would do research into what a potential client liked to eat and how they liked things cooked. We did this research together, just like I would research case law. We showed the clients we cared enough to do our homework, and we knew about the dietary needs of the client. If we went the normal route, it would not have been as good of a meeting, and it would not be the best use of everyone's time. Do it right the first time or don't do it at all (and make sure you have someone as awesome as Uncle Michael Chef on your side).

Getting back to the area of law I like the most (other than the business of law), I often attend mediations (as an attorney and as a mediator). Most of the time, people don't care where I went to school, how long I have been at this and boring things about me. They want to know what to expect, what are the rules and how quickly we can "get it done." So to spend thirty minutes on who I am is a waste, as no one really cares.

Now, there are times when people are so nervous that I will break the ice and make them feel comfortable. Crack a joke, make a comment about me, tell them to relax and let them know this is not the end-all be-all unless they want it to be. That will often save the day for them and let them relax and participate with less stress than was needed. Know the audience, read the room, and make everyone feel like they belong and fit in. I know I have been the round peg in the square hole my entire life, and I love living there. But most people like to just fit in, so remember that.

Another example is that you need to know how (and feel confident enough) to coach a client on what to say, how to dress and where to be in meetings. If your client is going to attend mediation via Zoom, and his or her background has expensive art and memorabilia, you cannot allow the client to say that he or she does not have financial resources or is not doing well in business. You want a simple and clear background. Artwork from your kids, closed shades and nothing fancy. Don't flaunt how much you have, unless your strategy is to have the other side think you have unlimited resources and will bury them in legal costs and fees. That strategy does not often work, but I hear it all the time.

When I worked in the foreclosure defense arena and a client would show up to court with a $10,000.00 watch and a thick gold chain, I would tell him to put all of the flashy things in his pocket or bag. How can you tell a judge you have no money to pay your mortgage, but you have $20,000 of jewelry on you (and it is so obvious that the judge can see it). Know your audience and know the setting. I am not suggesting that you ever be less than sincere or that you try to fool the court.

But there is no reason for your client (and more than likely, you) to look foolish when you are seeking help!

When I was trying to muster up some business and make some contacts with some of my fellow lacrosse dads, my choice of beer (and I really do not drink) was more important than how I dressed. When I met with dance dads and went to the dance shows, it was important that I had flowers for my daughter (it made me fit in with the other dads who knew the drill, and it made Madison happy).

When I travel, I make sure to bring Longpole Life and Longpole 4 Life stuff like hats, stickers, socks, and shirts and a good book that I am reading or think others should read. Why? Great conversation starters. Also, I can pass some of the stuff around, and I am always willing to give the book away as long as my contact information is already on the inside of the front cover. The stickers I hand out always have information on www.longpolelife.com, www.longpole4life.com, and/or www.mylazywear.com depending on the audience.

Now, sometimes, you want to impress a client. When I was going to an event that had former and current professional athletes, I made sure the car I was driving (either an Escalade or a Range Rover) was clean and looked good. I wanted them to see I care about my things, I take pride in looking good, and I have been successful enough to have a nice car. I will admit I am a car buff, and I love to drive a nice car (not to impress others, but to impress myself and to feel safe when I am on the South Florida roads). Would I drive my gas guzzler SUV to a fundraiser for the environment? No. Would I wear my NY Yankees shirt to a concert with a client who I am trying to impress who is a Red Sox fan? NO. You need to do your research and know your audience.

Find a common thread and be relatable. People want to work with people they mesh with and like on a personal level. We spend so much time working, and it makes it so much more enjoyable to work with people you actually know and like.

Some of my clients love watches, so I wear my old school TAG watch. Two of my clients only drink water, so each time I meet with them, I bring Fuji or Liquid Death. I know one of my clients has a daughter who loves art, so each time I see him, I bring markers or colored pencils. One client of mine cannot figure out how to use the redline feature in Word so I have to convert the document to PDF and then send it. I had a boss who only allowed people at the firm to use yellow highlighters and would refuse to review case law with highlighting on any other color. Again, it is so important to know your audience.

Who is your target? What does he or she like? You better know the answers to these questions before you show up.

I would suggest a cheat sheet like the one I started for you on the next page. Feel free to make it your own and adjust it as you deem fit, but this can be a good starting point.

Client Name	Contact Information	Notes (kids names, things liked by client, family, food)	What have given in the past	What want to give and when

CHAPTER 8

Don't Have that Knee Jerk Reaction

I need to make sure that I do not only write about this one, but also live it. It is not easy and is often hard to handle, but I know I need to make sure I continue to take my own advice on this one, and I have a few safeguards put in place. What do I mean?

Picture this, you get an email or a voicemail, and it gets you heated. It hit a nerve or felt like a personal attack (or just pissed you off). Whatever the email or the call is, you know exactly what I am talking about. It is from an opposing counsel, a client, the Court (even a kid or a spouse). It just gets your blood boiling, and you are pissed. So, you explode and pick up the phone to return the call or you write back an equally explosive or nasty email or text. BEFORE YOU HIT SEND or before you pick up the phone, take a second (like Joey Tribbiani from Friends when he did his "smell the fart" acting and took a deep breath when he forgot his lines) and breathe. Breathe in, breathe out. Do it a few times. Gather your thoughts. Cool off. Go for a walk. Woosa. Take control and stay calm. The anger will not do you any good.

Often, less is better. I recall two situations where this worked out (and I was able to teach in those moments). Many years back, I worked with a paralegal who was very invested in a case we were working on. She loved this specific case, cared deeply about the client and she was on a mission to win. We were representing an older woman who lost her husband, and the "evil" bank was trying to foreclose on her home. She was current on all her payments, made them all timely, but since her husband was deceased, the bank called the mortgage as due. She paid the full amount, and they sued her anyway. Yes, you read that correctly.

Anyway, this ambitious paralegal came to Court with me. The Court asked us to announce ourselves, and I introduced myself and the paralegal. The other side introduced herself, and the Court directed its attention to the opposing counsel. I know the Court was not happy because the opposing counsel was twenty minutes late (so that was strike one for her), but the Court drilled her and asked her twenty to thirty minutes of questions. Was there time for me to jump in and add facts in my client's favor? Yes. Would it have helped? Nope. I literally stood at the podium with my hands behind my back and kept making motions with my hands to let the paralegal know, relax, relax, this is going in our favor.

The hearing ended, and we won. What did I do to win? Nothing other than introducing myself and the paralegal and thanking the Court for its time. I could have jumped in numerous times and argued with opposing counsel (and it took great restraint to stand in silence), but this was a situation where saying nothing was the way to go. Fight off that need to speak and just let it go (once again, an Elsa reference).

The second example was much more recent (about three months prior to my writing this book). My opposing counsel on a case (we can call him Walt) sent me an email on a weekend telling me about the case, his position and how he was going to drag the case out and cost my client a ton of money.

Walt told me that if my client were to just settle for what he demanded, my client could save time, energy, embarrassment and money. It was not even a few hours later, still on the weekend, when Walt emailed me again and told me that I should really advise my client to take the offer, as it would be in my client's best interest. Like I explained in Chapter 6, unless it is urgent or time sensitive, I will more than likely wait until Monday after 8:30am to share an email like the one Walt sent. I go ten hours without responding to Walt (when, in actuality, I drafted a proposed response for Walt, which I will explain below, but did not send it out yet).

Guess what? I got not one, but two more emails from Walt. He went from a demand of about $28,000.00 to $3,500.00 in the matter of a few hours, without a single response from me or my client. I broke my own rule and sent the emails to my client, and my client told me to keep letting Walt negotiate against himself. Well, guess what, when I woke up Monday, I had an additional email where Walt lowered the demand again.

This time, I picked up the phone, called Walt, and asked him why he was doing what he was doing. His response was that I was "ignoring him and he wanted to get my attention," which made no sense to me. If I wanted to do that tactic, I would have increased my demand from $28,000 to $30,000.00 and moved upward. But hey, "he knows what he is doing."

The parties did eventually reach an agreement and resolved their differences by entering into a confidential settlement agreement. All I am permitted to say is that a settlement agreement was reached between the parties and the terms are confidential. Winner winner, chicken dinner! Happy client. Happy Jason and one less case to handle. To this day, I still have no clue what Walt was doing (and I do not think Walt knew, either).

I mentioned above that I sent an email to myself before I sent it to Walt. I often send emails to ME and ONLY me (or I will send it to someone I work with for him or her to review). I then leave it in my inbox and come back to it later (in a few minutes, hours, or even the next day). Why? I allow the anger to calm so I can read it in a better mindset, with less emotion swirling (which also gets me back into the chapter of this book "It Will Be Personal"). It is rare that I will send the email as written, and I remove some of the things I thought I wanted to send but made the decision not to send. The knee jerk reaction might have felt good at the time but will, more often than not, come back to bite you in the a$$. Plus, I think it is important to have a second set of eyes on things, even if it is my own eyes. Trust me, this has helped me avoid unnecessary conflict. Take the time to not send it; you will be happier in the long run.

I guess the question is how do we balance this with the need to get things done and not put things off? I wish there was a failproof way I could share. I recommend that you follow the above, but you need to make it work for you. There is no precise answer (which is why it is called the Practice of Law, like I covered in the earlier chapter, "It is Called the Practice of Law for a Reason"). Try things, see what works and what does not. If it works, run with it. If it does not, try again. If some of it works, then see what you can do slightly differently. This is an ongoing process and will not happen overnight, so play around and see what works. I do know that a slight pause or break will more often than not be the way to go.

One additional thought: when you do feel like you want to yell and scream or just want to attack, just STOP!!! Take a walk, play a game on your phone, check some reels on social media, drink water, breathe, go for a run… I would avoid more caffeine, and I would avoid a sugar rush, but do what it is that helps calm you. You got this!!

CHAPTER 9

Own Up to Your Mistakes

No one, and I mean no one, is perfect. You might look up to people who do what you want to do the way you want to do it, you may have mentors, you may have idols, you may have people you want to be like, but trust me, no one is perfect. We ALL make mistakes. It is how we handle these mistakes and move forward from them that defines us as human beings.

I recently had a great talk with Marc Nudelberg, and he told me about his 24-hour rule. What is that? My interpretation of it (again, this is what I took away from the conversation) is that if he had a bad day or made a mistake, he does not dwell on it for more than a day. He allows himself a set amount of time to beat himself up and to reflect on the situation, and then the next day is a new day and a fresh start. It is an incredible concept. Admittedly, I am working on that for myself, and let me tell you, it is not easy, but I am getting better.

Another thing I learned is it is not how many times you fall down, but it is HOW you get back up. If you get up ready to be knocked down again, then you are deflated and defeated, and you need to stop. STOP NOW!!! You need to be ready to get up and go. You learned what did not work, and now you can try again, but differently.

There is a line from *National Treasure* (I love that movie and watched again last night), and the character Ben Gates talks about how Thomas Edison failed 2,000 times when he made the light bulb. Edison did not see it as he failed 2,000 times, but rather, he found 2,000 ways to not make a light bulb. Think about that. We do not learn from our successes; we learn from failure and adversity. If all was peachy keen and you had no adversity or challenges, you would just coast though life. But with challenges, we learn what works, what does not work, and how to do things differently.

Okay, so back to confessing to mistakes. When I make a mistake, I do not just say, "I screwed up, now what?". I say, "Okay, I screwed up, how can I fix it?" I don't just let things sit and fester. I take a deep breath, gain my composure, and see what I can do to right the ship.

I don't say, "Okay, I filed it late, Oh well, we will see what happens." I call the JA or the chambers of the judge, and I explain the blunder. I ask if I file a motion asking for an extension *nunc pro tunc* (a Latin phrase that means "now for then" and is used to correct a mistake as if it were made in the original (so kind of like back dating it)), would the court consider it (and hopefully grant it). I have the motion ready to go and I file it. Again, get proactive and own up to your mistakes (or try to resolve them ASAP or at least get ahead of them).

I also believe that what people want is communication. If you tell people what you are doing, they know what to expect. I am in the college recruiting phase of life with my 16-year-old son. He is a Longpole Defender in lacrosse, and he has been to numerous colleges to try to see if he is a fit for their lacrosse program and if the school is a fit for him academically. We truly respect the coaching staff that tells him, "Hey, you are on our board, but not a top pick," or "Hey, you are a good player, but we are not going to be extending you an offer." We would rather know where we stand instead of hearing, "We like you and we will be in touch" (and the phone does not ring).

Think back to when you applied for something (job, college, law school, a raffle, an auction, etc.) and you found out you did not get it. Although the news was not what you wanted to hear, you have to admit it was better than not knowing. I know (trust me, I know) when you are in the moment, things do not make sense (and it often sucks), but there is something to be learned. So, make mistakes, own up to them, fix them, and learn from them. It is all part of life. You live and you learn (and just make sure you avoid making the same mistakes over and over).

I am once again on another flight (this time to Philly), and the flight was delayed due to a mechanical issue with the plane. People lined up to ask what was wrong with the plane and what the next steps were. The people working at the counter were not very communicative, and my fellow passengers were getting very angry. All they wanted was an update, status, some form of communication.

I told that to one guy working at the counter and he told me, "Thank you." I think when a bunch of people around me heard that and told him all they wanted was to be updated, he got the message. Every fifteen minutes or so, he would announce the status and the next steps. Guess what, even though the announcement was that we were waiting on a new tire for the plane to arrive and be installed, that went a long way to get cooperation from the passengers (and gave the people at the counter more time to do other things like help people get different connecting flights). We got on the plane about two hours later, and there was no angry mob. Everyone was calm (I am not gonna say happy, but calm). Communication is key!

CHAPTER 10

The One Business Day Rule

Society today is all about the now. What can you do now? No one wants to wait. Not for food, not for movies, not for answers, emails, calls, texts . . . nothing. We are the quick fix, need-it-now society. How can we deal with that as professionals and keep our sanity (or just have lives)?

I like the one-business-day rule. You can implement it any way you want, and I give you complete freedom to edit this rule as it suits you. The gist of it is that you will respond to any email, call or text (or any other way you are contacted) within a set time period. I know attorneys who include information in their signature block that if you do not hear back from them in one business day, email them again because there is a chance that she or he did not get it. The attorney sets reasonable expectations, and clients are satisfied with getting a response or knowing what is going on (and a possible recommended follow-up). I know I communicate this well in emails and have signature blocks set for things like time Out of Office (OOO), office closures, and holidays. People want to be in the know, and it is simple to accomplish that.

The movie *Be Cool* made reference to this and hit this well out of the park. The character, Elliot (played by the Rock), asked Chilly Palmer (played by John Travolta), "When are you gonna call me?" The best response ever was, "When your phone rings." Think about that!!!! Mic Drop moment. I love that! The sarcasm and the directness are priceless.

But at the same time, it is not the answer that clients would want to hear. Remember, they are paying you, so you do owe them a duty and communication. Why not just tell them when to expect to hear from you? One business day, forty-eight hours, the next day, evenings, whatever works for you, just communicate and it will work. That is the key: communication.

If you tell people what to expect and you stick to it (or do better), they will be happy. I do this all the time, and it works wonders. I had that conversation today with a client. "If I get you something by the end of the week, would that suffice?" The answer was yes. I know my own goal was to shoot for Thursday evening or Friday morning. But if it takes until the end of the week, I am still golden. Your communication and setting of expectations is often better than any other response you could give. I am an over-communicator (or as my wife and kids would say, an over-sharer). But I know when I share what to expect, and sometimes even explain why it will be delayed or not as fast as someone would want, it works.

I work with one gentleman, who I will call Seth. Seth always needs everything yesterday, and everything is urgent, critical, and cannot wait. "I can have it done in three days" is not an answer Seth wants to hear. Here is where I digress for a moment. Often, when Seth needs it right away, he is the cause of the urgency. He sat on a contract for multiple days, and when he got it to me, it was a rush. "Not my issue," is what I keep telling myself.

I live by the motto that your lack of preparation and diligence does not make it an emergency for me. Nope, not happening. Second, I often hear from Seth that "it will only take you thirty to forty-five minutes to get it done, so please, can you just stop what you are doing and help?". Ummm, no! Although the task might only take an hour or two (as it never is a thirty to forty-five minute project or review), that means I need to put someone else's time sensitive work aside and put his first. Not happening. I will admit that if Seth were to ask me to stop working on Project A for him and work on Project B instead, I would not object to that, but you cannot constantly put out fires and allow people to skip the line.

Think about the last time you were waiting and someone skipped or cut the line. How did that make you feel? I know when I am on the dance line picking up Madison and cars skip ahead of me, well, let's just say it does not make me happy. I bite my tongue and sit tight as I do not want to embarrass her.

However, I need to tell ya that in my professional experience, Thursday afternoons are the best (insert sarcasm). That is when all of the corporate clients want to clear their desks and To Do Lists for the weekend. How can they do that with ease? Send things to legal. That gets it off their desks, and the expectation is that you, the attorney, will jump on it and get it done. "It is only twelve pages, and that's short." Yes, but I have seven documents ahead of yours (three of them happen to be for you). Come on now, seriously?

I am at the stage in my career (and have a good rapport with my clients) where I can call these bozos out and tell them, "Thanks for this new contract, I will have back to you Wednesday." If they don't like it, then they can ask for it sooner. If I hear nothing, then the goal is what I set. Again, learn how to set boundaries and set these boundaries (I know it is easier said than done, but start NOW). You will thank me in years to come (or maybe even days to come).

The other thing that I can pass on is to under promise and overdeliver (or build in time for you). What does that mean? If you want to try to get something done by Thursday, then tell the client Friday. You can send it Friday (or Thursday) if you want, but you will have completed the task in a timely fashion. You can also build in time for you. For example, when I am leaving for a trip and coming back, I tell people I am gone a day earlier and coming back a day later. Why? I now have some flex time to respond to emails and calls, unpack and unwind. I build a "To Do" list and start checking things off (that is very cathartic to me, helps my brain function and helps me remain calm).

CHAPTER 11

You Be You- What Works for Others May Not Work for You

During COVID, my daughter, Madison, showed me how her brain works. She is smart, meticulous and needs everything to be done a certain way. She enabled me to see how to do things my way for me. She told me, "Dad, You Be You!" I loved that and even posted on LinkedIn about it (and shared her artwork where she made a magnet on a small tile for me, which I still have on my file cabinet in my office). "You Be You" hit me hard on so many levels. What works for me may not work for you and may not work for another person. But be true to you, and be open to learning and accepting others and the ways they want to do things.

My eyes were really opened to this on two separate occasions. The first was when my grandmother died. We had an awesome person and attorney handle her estate (it was not anything significant, but she did own a condo and a car and she had more than one heir). My Dad called me up and asked me if I could call the attorney who was handling the estate and ask him three questions. I said of course, got the three questions, and made the call.

Later on in the day, I called my Dad with the answers to the questions and filled him in. Right after I hung up with my Dad, I called my Dad back and asked him why I needed to make the call for him. He told me that when I spoke with the attorney, he saw on a bill there was a phone call and a "No Charge." When my Dad called the attorney, the call was billed for (and my Dad was very happy with the friends and family rate on the bills and the work that was done, but he liked "no charge" more than a discounted charge).

I learned from that, and one of the practices that we implement at the firm is that we do not charge for routine calls. We enter the time on the bill and "no charge". Why? Well #1, I learned from my Dad. #2, I like when a client says, let me call Jason and ask before I make a decision or sign an agreement. It is easier to help before there is a signed agreement (or a potential problem after the signing of an agreement). Clients know they will not pay for that call, so there is no financial downside to calling me. Plus, clients feel they can call and speak to me without getting dinged on a bill. It builds trust and rapport and encourages communication between me and my clients. #3, it is also a record for the client to see I am working on the file. If you just make calls and do not have a record of it, it can be disastrous.

The second time my eyes were opened was when I needed to retain an attorney to assist me on a matter for me and the firm. When I would send an email or make a call and would not hear back right away (or "soon enough"), it would tick me off. I would think the worst, or I would feel like I was not getting the love and the attention I wanted (and was paying for). I sat at my desk distracted from the rest of my day, and I was annoyed (and a real "pleasure" to be around).

Learning from this and seeing it firsthand, I made sure to implement the "One Business Day Rule", which I covered in the prior chapter. I want my clients (and friends) to feel like I have their best interests in mind, I can be reached and I am ready to help (and not just say it but show it).

Currently, I am a bit behind on that right now, but there are exceptions to every rule (my Dad is presently in the ICU in Atlanta, and I am still about two days behind). To make sure I am communicative to clients (and the court and opposing counsels), I have an OOO (out of office signature block in place) to let people know I am OOO on a family matter and to please excuse delayed responses. Does this solve all issues? No, but I feel like it is the right thing to do (and it ties in well with Chapter 6, where we cover the question of what would your Mother, Rabbi, or Priest say).

So, how can you, as a newer attorney (or even as a seasoned attorney), learn here? What is the lesson? What is Jason babbling about (like, come on dude, what are you trying to say)?

I tell people all the time: find someone who does what you do and see how you get treated. If you own a restaurant, go eat at a similar restaurant and see what they do to your liking and what they don't. Go see a doctor and see how long you sit in the waiting room and wait for your appointment. If you own a car dealership, go check out the sales team and customer service department at another dealership. Hire an attorney to represent you in a matter (or just go in for a consultation). See what you like, and see how you are treated. Learn from it. It is research, and I am sure you will see things that they do great that you can implement or see things that are not so great that you know you can do better (or how you can do them better).

You need to see, and you need a base line so you can compare. When you have things the way you want them (or see progression in the right direction), then you are on your way. It is all about learning, growing, and seeing what works and what does not. Give it a shot and see.

CHAPTER 12

PPP

Now that the world has been through the pandemic, all business owners (and most of the general public) know about PPP. Paycheck Protection Program. PPP helped me and the firm get through some tough months and allowed us to stay in business (which was the purpose of PPP). It was GREAT, and we are thankful for it as it allowed us to keep the status quo (and allowed people who worked with us to get paid and be able to handle their own financial situations).

What the world does not know is that I have been using my own form of PPP before COVID was ever thought of. My PPP was developed by my wife, Tova.

PPP means Plan, Prepare and Perform. It came into existence when I had my first mock trial in law school and Tova was kind enough to be a witness. My partner, Brian Griper, and I used Plan, Prepare and Perform to set out the motive of the defendant. We were the State Attorneys (also called the Prosecutors), and we established our case by using PPP – Plan, Prepare and Perform! The defendant planned his crime out, he prepared for it and then he performed the crime (in this case, it was a murder). We used this theory throughout the entire case, and the panel of volunteer judges (made up of attorneys and actual sitting judges), advised us that they loved the theme running through the entire case.

This carried over to my life, my practice, and my family. We all Plan, Prepare and Perform as a family (and a firm). We Plan for the day, the week, the school year. We have a family meeting every Sunday night where we go through the week ahead and make sure we can all be on the same page and be there for one another (as of the writing of this book, Madison does not drive, and Logan has access to a vehicle so he can help). We do not have a white board that we use anymore (the kids like their phone calendars, and Tova and I like our small day planners). We can all plan out the week.

For the firm, we would meet at least one time a week (usually Tuesday) to go over the rest of the week and the following week. This got us on the same page and made sure we all planned for the next ten days or so and would be able to support each other.

How do you Prepare? I know in my house we all prepare each evening for the next day. Pick out clothing, gather snacks and do what needs to be done. I know I put in my time, prepare a "To Do List" for the next day and the rest of the week, and I add anything I did not accomplish in the current day to the next day (or days). I prepare for the next few days. I know when I see my lists over and over, they put my mind at ease. It reminds me of what I need to do, and at the same time, it allows me to have some peace.

My entire life (right or wrong), I have lived preparing for the worst and hoping for the best. I mean, that is why we all have insurance or rainy-day funds, right? I know it is not the happy-go-lucky attitude I wish I had, but it is what it is. I have learned how to manage it, and most of the time, I am no longer waiting for the other shoe to drop (as there was a time when I could not be in the moment because I was waiting).

To me, Perform is the easiest one of the three. You go out and do what you planned and prepared for. I go into a deposition, I attend a hearing, I write a pleading. I do what needs to be done. It is like when an athlete, entertainer, musician, performer, or some other person practices non-stop for the big event of the game or the show. All you have done up until now was for the sole purpose of the show or the big game (or in my case, the big hearing or mediation). This is the time to shine. Go crush it!

One other thing that I cannot stress to you enough, which is covered in the previous chapter, is to remember that what works for you may not work for others. Combine that into PPP, and you will be a rock star (or golden).

For example, I know I work better at different times of the day for various tasks. I like to write (this book included) when I am sitting in airports, on airplanes, or when traveling. I am not sure why, maybe it is that I am still "working" when I am away, but it is not really work for me (see Chapter 18). I know when I need to draft a long brief or tackle discovery, I need to be in the office so that I can pace without bothering others. I cannot sit still, and I need space to walk. When I am on phone calls where I do not need to take notes, I like to do it in the late AM or afternoon so that I can put in my ear buds and walk and talk. If I have a filing due, I like when it is done between 3pm and 4pm (early enough in case there are technical issues, but late enough so I was able to think about it and make any last-minute edits or additions). Again, find what works for you, and then you can follow PPP.

How can I plan, prepare, and perform in lawyer-ese? You have a new possible client call you, and she wants to meet to discuss her case. You plan for the meeting, and you prepare. You have the conference room ready, cold drinks and a retainer letter ready to go. You might be high tech and have your laptop connected to a big screen television. Then, you Perform. You wow the client and get the retainer! PPP at its finest. Nicely done. So now what?? You need to continue to Perform and make sure the client is happy.

Let me give you another example. When I am traveling (which, these days, seems to be weekly, or like eight flights in nine days), I need to chew gum and listen to music on the way up and the way down. If I do not do this, then my ears become clogged, and I am an unhappy camper. I know when I have gum in packs with wrappers, I am prepared as I keep the wrapper and put the chewed gum in it when we are in the air or when we land. But when I have the gum that comes in a cup or a pouch, I am often stuck chewing longer than I hoped for, as I have nowhere to throw out the gum (and I will not dispose of it improperly, as that sucks when you step in gum or something is sticky). So, for all of you gum chewers, I have helped you prepare for your trip in case you do not have something to put your gum in – the last page of this chapter is reserved for you to tear away parts to throw out your gum. Literally. I know it is kind of silly, but it gets the point across. PPP!

One thing to keep in mind: no matter how well you implement the PPP mantra, there will be things you can never plan for. While I was writing this book, my Dad, Bruce, suffered from a cardiac event midflight on an airplane flying from Germany to Atlanta, Georgia (and then was supposed to continue on to West Palm Beach, Florida). Nothing I could have done ever would have helped me plan, prepare and perform for that. Nothing.

My Dad had all of this occur on October 9, 2023, and he passed away on Halloween 2023 (October 31, 2023). He fought the good fight (like he always did), but it was too much stress and trauma on his body (he was brought back to life three times in a short period of time). He is an amazing man who was loved by everyone he encountered. He lived a full life without regret. I guess the lesson here is simple: you can do your best to be a planner (like my Dad was), and you need to just make sure you plan for the unexpected and roll with it or alter your plan and live life to the fullest and enjoy every moment.

Never in a million years would I have ever thought I would be where I am at this exact moment in time. I am sitting in the last row of a plane (Row 38, at least it is an aisle) next to my mom flying home from Atlanta with my Dad being flown home later tonight in the belly of a plane. I never planned or prepared for this, but I did perform as a son, husband, father, brother, nephew and a person. My brothers and I were able to be there for my mom in our own ways, as was my mother-in-law, Rina, who was the only bright spot in an otherwise horrible series of days. Rina and my mom were roomies (as Madison says), and Rina was the support my mom needed when she and my dad were stuck in Atlanta. Rina made sure my mom had a place to stay, food to eat, and mental support. Rina was the PPP-er and is the true definition of a person putting family over everything. No task is too big for family. Rina not only says it, but she means it and shows it. I know Rina told me to stop saying thank you, but I wanted to say one more thank you from me, Mom, and Dad.

To sum it up, implement the Plan, Prepare, and Perform mantra, and go for it. But keep your head up and keep at it if you need to alter things as needed. Nothing in life is perfect, and you do the best you can with what you have. I know you will be happy you prepared. Remember, luck seems to find the people who Plan, Prepare and then Perform.

BLANK PAGE
FOR GUM

CHAPTER 13

Snowballs

I know when you are right out of school and eager to have your own clients and have your name on the door, all that stands in your way is getting your own book of business. I went into this in Chapter 2. I recall when I was a young attorney, all I wanted was clients of my own. I would be able to earn more, run files and cases the way I wanted and be only beholden to the client and the billing department (as what was on the bills needed to be collected and accounted for).

I wanted to know how to do it, but what was the secret? I saw attorneys at small firms with million-dollar books of business and other attorneys at big firms with five-million-dollar books of business. But how?? Can I do this? I was confident that I could, but I needed to know what the formula was or how I should start. I needed my own tour guide (or mentor) to show me.

I remember sitting with other newer attorneys and associates at lunches in downtown Fort Lauderdale where we all discussed this (and let me tell you, the food was good and the company was better, but the increased waist size of my pants and the financial cost hurt). I was even at a great law firm that paid to have us go to Chicago to learn how to generate business. We learned about things such as "Hidden Treasures" and how you can find a client anywhere.

I had one partner that I worked for who told me to just keep at it. It will happen. Once you land a decent client and do good work, then it will snowball into more and more. He was not talking about the family member for whom you go to court to handle a speeding ticket or the neighbor who you help with setting up a corporation. I am talking about the client who needs your help and picks you for you.

You need to treat this client like gold (I mean, treat all clients like gold, but for this one, go the extra mile). Why? One client will snowball into two and then to four and then six and so on and so on.

I was called the other day and asked about my firm's marketing budget. I told the person it was $650.00 before COVID, and now it is $150.00. The first question out of his mouth was, "Why did you cut the budget by $500.00 per month?" I laughed and said, "My bad, the budget was annual, not monthly," and there was silence on the other end of the phone.

When my kids were in elementary school, I put up a banner at the school for $500.00 a year, and I would spend about $150.00 per year on pens to give out to clients and to leave at restaurants. They were not fancy pens, but rather pens that stood out. They are orange and black, and they were so reasonably priced that I left them everywhere I would go.

I still have handfuls of them at my office (and to this day, my mom tells me they are her favorite pens). I admit that I did order fancier pens in 2022, and I am less inclined to just leave them places, but the marketing budget is not much higher than the $150.00 per month.

I get my clients by putting my money where my mouth is. We pride ourselves on doing the best work we can, being responsive and not over-billing. We treat clients the way we want to be treated. I know I have done consultations, and at the end of the meeting, I was offered $300.00 or $500.00 for the meeting. I have turned it down (unless it was discussed before the meeting ever happened). The first words out of that potential client's mouth (after "thank you") is, "I have a friend who needs an attorney" or "I have another matter that I would like your help with."

So that meeting and turning away a few dollars results in clients and the best advertising you would ever get – Word of Mouth! Do well and let them sing your praises. It is the best form of marketing and advertising you could ever have. One client, to two, to twenty, to the sky is the limit. You are on your way!

CHAPTER 14

Form Your Own Board

I hear it all the time: "I have a mentor" or "I have a role model" or "I work with a Coach." GREAT! I have all of these things, and they form my support network (or as some people would say, my own personal Advisory Board). I personally call it a Sounding Board. What is that and what does that mean?

I have the people I go to for certain things. For example, for legal help, John Bradley and Joel Rothman are my first two calls. For food ideas and moral support, Uncle Michael Chef. Movies, TV, music, Apple questions and just to feel good about myself, I call Josh Gordon. I can go on and on with specific things that specific people do for me to support me, love me and help me. I have my own Board of these amazing people. Create one for yourself (and feel free to use the chart at the end of the chapter to get you started). There are so many variations you can use, so nothing is set in stone.

Some people I have been coached by suggest doing this with clients as well. But you should rank clients by how they relate to your business.

For example, Randy is a connector, and I know if I need to meet someone, chances are that Randy will have the connection and can do the introduction. He is also the guru of follow ups and knows how to make people feel special. Therefore, I would have Randy in my sample chart below and make those notes. I could rank Randy as an "A" or as a "Connector," as he would be awesome for me in almost any setting. He can help me meet people, schmooze them to try to gain them as clients, and follow up with them to stay top of mind.

Max, my buddy of a long, long time (who is a tremendous deal maker and attorney) is a good person to figure things out with and could help me determine how to work a deal and make money. Max would walk through a wall of fire for me, but I know he is not the follow up guy. He would not be a "Connector," but he can still be an "A".

I could go on and on, but the point is to just figure out where the people in your life belong. Your brother could be just your brother, but he could also be much more. Each person is different, and when you know what role they fill, you will be happy.

Another example is David Block, who I have mentioned a lot thus far. I know David would do anything in his power if I asked (or even needed and did not ask). But I also know that if I need to remember a date or need to make sure something gets mailed or sent out in a timely manner, he is not the guy to remind me. I try to help David remember things, as that not his strength. But if I ever needed anything, David would be the guy who would pick me up on the side of the road if my car broke down. Heck, David was the first person to send something to my house when Dad passed.

Uncle Milic is another one on the Board. I know if I need anything, he would make it happen. No questions asked, just consider it done. I think you get the point, and I will not keep going.

Not everyone on your Board needs a specific role or category, but I would suggest you try to give them one. If you cannot "sort them out" or "figure out where he or she fits," then just have the name on there, and I am sure you can supplement or edit in time.

Also, don't feel you need to put everyone in your life on the Board or that the Board is set in stone. I know I have added, subtracted and edited the people on my Board. Any given week, month, or year, this can change. It is okay to have a Board meeting (all by yourself) to see who you want to stay on the Board and who has fulfilled his or her purpose.

We have the right, freedom and responsibility to keep things fluid and current. You don't need to keep your college roommate on the Board just because. If you no longer really connect with him or her, or if your relationship has changed over time, it is okay to remove him or her from your Board. That does not mean he or she is no longer important to you, just that his or her role has changed.

This Board is about you. For example, my Board consists of a business coach, an attorney with more experience that me, a close friend who has a law degree but does not practice, an attorney with less experience than me, a marketing guru, Gus, Dr. Bogart, Uncle Milic, my wife, a mentor, Chef, Uncle Doodie, my kids, and my mom. Ask me in a few months, and there can be some changes, but this is my current brain trust. These are the people I can go to for advice, use as a sounding board, or just rely on for anything. They are MY Board!

Another thing is to find out what they like, who they know and how they like to be contacted. Uncle Milic loves flat water, to be contacted via text and for the holidays likes to be given things from my kids. Gus likes flat water, hates getting gifts, is good via email and text and appreciates anything you get for his family (just do not get him anything big or expensive). It is a good thing to know and to keep track of.

I have an example of the chart I use below in case you want to see what I do. You might think this is overkill and too much. There is no right answer, but I found this helped me (especially during gift giving time – which I cover in Chapter 16), and it supports what I have learned and set forth in Chapter 16.

Name	Strengths	Best way to contact	People they know who I want to know	Things they like/ gifts	Notes/ Misc.

CHAPTER 15

Book Time for You

As attorneys, one of the skills I think we need to develop and strengthen (and have as a superpower) is organization. People talk about blocking time or following an agenda. If you are not good at things like that, then you can use an alarm on your phone or have someone help you with it. Reminders, post-its, the annoying alarm on your phone all work. There is no right answer, but I have provided some various suggestions and invite you to find what works for you.

I know I personally plan things out each Sunday evening for the upcoming week (as I covered in Chapter 12), but one thing I failed to mention was that you need to book time for you! I AM GUILTY OF NOT FOLLOWING MY OWN ADVICE HERE. I am not going to even try to fake it or convince you that I do this well because I don't. What I do well is book time for my family, but for me, not so much. I am working on it daily and getting better at it, but I am still not a pro (or good at it).

I will give you an example. A typical Thursday for me goes like this:

6:20AM: wake up and make sure Madison is awake (90% of the time, she is)

7:00AM: wake myself again, check on Madison, make sure Logan is awake and help them get out of the house for school

7:45AM – 8:30AM: check emails and respond to same

8:30AM: check in with mom (to say hello) and call my friend and client

9AM: call with client in NY

10:30AM -11AM: weekly check-in with real estate client

11AM – 11:50AM: call with my coach Judi

11:55AM – 12:45PM: host podcast/radio show "Ask Jason Weiss"

12:45PM-1:45PM: attend weekly group meeting to discuss profit strategies

4PM: weekly call with client to discuss current pending cases

5:30PM – 6PM: Accountability coach call

6:30PM: Dinner with family

What do I do with the limited "open" time between the meetings and the calls? Work. I work on cases, files, pleadings, emails, etc. What is not on that list? Time for me. I need to begin making an entry that would be for me, like "9:30-10AM, write my book, walk, run, garden or do something else for me." I fail miserably in doing that. I carve out some time on the weekends when I am not in the Northeast at a lacrosse event or game, but it is not consistent and regular like it needs to be.

I need to pay attention to it.

When my sunflowers begin to wilt, I give them water and love, so why not do the same for myself? I am working on taking a few hours a week for me (I am not trying, as that word is too much of an excuse, so I am doing it). I play a game on my phone, watch a game or a movie, play Ms. Pacman, write some of a book (this one or part two that I have already begun to outline). Something for me.

When my mom and brother told me Dad had passed (despite my seeing him three days earlier), I was able to put Family Over Everything (#FOE – thanks Steve Nudelberg) and get on a plane to be with my mom for the start of this new step. I put work, cases, stresses, and BS that was so not important aside, and I was able to be there for my mom and my family.

I took off today (Wednesday) as a travel day, and then I will be off Friday through Tuesday night for the funeral and Shiva. I decided that it was best for me to work a little Thursday, and my mom, Rabbi, wife, mother-in-law, and kids all said that was okay. I listened to my own advice by asking my Rabbi and mother and putting family over everything (and you should listen as well and not use a tragic life event to make you realize that).

I also have my Dad whispering in my ear one question – "Can it wait?" If it can, then let it wait. But no matter what, I am going to follow what my Dad showed me my entire life: family first. It is always the right time for you to be with your family. I hear him saying, "Jason, you really need time for you and time with Tova and the kids. It is NOT you or the family; it is both YOU & FAMILY." Thanks, Dad, I got the message loud and clear.

My Dad practiced what he preached, as he would go to a movie on opening day by himself (by choice). He would "allow" my mom to take him for lunch and to drive him to the movies, and then he would go see a movie a second time with my kids. There was time for him, time for him and mom, and time with the grandkids he loved so so much! Three ways to spend time.

My time for me is going to get an adjustment by my close friend and chiropractor Dr. Bogart once a week, getting a haircut with Bobby every four weeks, and roaming Home Depot or Lowe's looking for plants and seeds or Wal-Mart looking for Legos (this is not a constant or regular event, but it is something I truly love doing. This is me time). I also have family time that I LOVE LOVE LOVE, but I do now have some set time for me time (a small amount, but a step in the right direction). So, plan some YOU time. Block it out now! Even if it is one hour a week, just get it on the books in Sharpie marker (not pencil).

Why is this so important? It may seem more than obvious, but often, we miss things (or cannot find things) that are staring us in the face. I do that with my reading glasses all the time, so I literally have twelve pairs of glasses in my cars, my house, my backpack and anywhere else I go. I know I will lose glasses and will not recall where I left them, so I planned, prepared and performed knowing this.

What I am really trying to say here is that if you do not take time for you, the burnout will come quickly. I know, I know, "It will never happen to me," but let me tell ya, it will. It can come in all shapes and sizes, and you might not even know it is happening.

It can be that you get on the scale and don't like what you see (guilty as charged). It can be that you have not gotten a haircut in multiple weeks and you look messy. It can be you are driving around with a nail in your tire or the check engine light is on but you "do not have time to get it fixed." It can be, "I am so busy that I do not have time to _____" (fill in the blank as it applies to you). It can be, "If X happens, then I can do Y" (I use this one all of the time).

This is all part of you needing to care for you and make time for you. That is not in my nature, as I feel I am a giver and not a taker, but I am making it a part of my life. Like they tell you on an airplane, you need to put on your mask to take care of yourself and then put it on the child who is traveling with you. You cannot help others if you cannot function.

Think about this. Your iPhone is more than likely a staple in your life and a necessity. You "need" it to make calls, send texts, check emails, watch movies, check out Instagram, to give to your kids to make them stop crying, and so on and so on. But the battery life (don't get me started on that one) will only last for so long without a charge. You need to think of yourself in that same light. Without taking time to charge yourself, you are going to be useless. The consequences of that will be detrimental to your life, your career, your health and so much more. When you plug in your phone, make sure you plug yourself in for a recharge as well. What you decide to do to fill up your cup is up to you, but make it about you.

Let me get you started. The next page is for doodles, notes, plans and just some notes for you. Put what you want on it. Color, draw, do math, make a to do list, use it for gum like in Chapter 12, but do something for you. You need it, and I assure you that you will thank yourself for doing it (and maybe me, too).

DOODLE SPACE

CHAPTER 16

Business is Personal

What does "business is personal" mean to you? To me, it means people want to do business with you (as an attorney or anything else you decide to do) because of you. They like your suit, your ads, your passion, your hair, your demeanor, your rates, your geographic location, and the list goes on. Although it is a business matter you are assisting with, the decision to work with you is personal. Get personal, as it is a good thing and is never a bad thing. We want to work with and be with people we like. You might not be inclined to be overly personal, but to show your personal side is a very good thing.

How can you do that? Find out about your client. When is her birthday? Does she have kids? When are her kids' birthdays? What are the kids into? What does she like? Where do they eat or travel? Find out personal things. Take notes. Get to know the person, not just the business.

We all like to work with people we like (and know), so be likable and get to know the people you do business with. My client was going out to dinner with his spouse for a wedding anniversary, and I casually asked where they were going. He told me, and I got Uncle Michael Chef to help me arrange an appetizer being sent to the table with a note saying, "Happy Anniversary." I have another client who was going on a Disney Cruise. His daughter loves the Princesses, so I had Uncle Doodie help me get the package so their room could be decorated in the Princess theme. He was over the moon appreciative (and it was the highlight of the trip for his daughter).

I also have a client (and friend) who, like me, has a daughter. For the holidays, I get him a little something, but I spend the majority of the money I want to spend on the gift for his daughter. She loves art, so we make sure to keep that in mind. However, one year we got her a Lego set, and although she loved it, my buddy told me if I ever got her another Lego set that he needs to build for her, he will drive to my house, pick me up and drive me to his house so I can build the Legos. Now me being me, I got him a small set (about 40 pieces) and told him he can build that with his daughter. I know one year, I am going to build a set and give it to him already done (or I might buy a big set so I need to go to his house to build it).

The point of this is that it is okay to get personal. People want to work with people they know, like and trust. Go connect and get personal!

Another thing that is awesome is handwritten notes. If you meet someone for the first time, many people will send an email or a text saying, "It was great to meet you, and I look forward to [some future event]." Now imagine this, you get a handwritten, personal note instead. Hmmm...

I know, as someone who is in the thick of the recruiting process with Logan, that Logan is great at sending the personal email or text as a follow up. But when he really wants to stand out, he will hand-write a note and send it via Federal Express. It adds a little something. In the sequel to this book, I hope to share how it worked and what came of all of it and announce where he decided to go to college. But this handwritten note, delivered via Federal Express, makes him stand out, and it shows he has real interest in the school. It is above and beyond the "norm" and very personal.

One additional thing you can do is invite a client to do something with you and your family. I have traveled with clients and their families. I am not saying to invite a client to an event and get her and her husband seats at a table at an event. But, "Hey, let's go to a game and get eight seats and sit together and tailgate." Or, "Come to my house for Thanksgiving or Madison Eve (we do not celebrate Christmas Eve in my house, but for the past fourteen years (by the time this book comes out), we do Madison Eve).

Show an interest in wanting to get to know people, and make business personal. Do not make people feel obligated to do something. Make it so they want to do something with you other than just business. Make them feel special, but make sure it is natural and not forced. You want to show up authentically.

I also know people like to get things in the US Mail. We still do holiday cards and gifts, but we do not send them around Christmas so they do not get lost in the shuffle. We now send cards and gifts in the middle of January. By then, people are back to the grind and in the office, and a card or a gift is a surprise and a cheerful event. It makes you stand out.

I know people who do not give gifts for the holidays and instead send a package for Valentine's Day, Thanksgiving, or some other less traditional gift giving time. In years past, I have sent gifts to dads on Father's Day, such as a hat or a lacrosse item. I have sent gifts to mothers on their kids' birthday, saying "Happy Birthing Day." There are so, so, so many ways to show up differently.

I am not the creator of these concepts, but I do make them my own. I would recommend getting to know Scott MacGregor and John Ruhlin and reading their books, following them on LinkedIn and just listening to pointers they offer. I would also like to recommend that you research Randy Ostrow. All three of these people are terrific idea guys who think outside the box and do things differently.

One additional point I cannot stress enough is that we all love praise. If someone did something great, you say thanks, and then you move on. When someone does something bad, you complain, you file a grievance, and you let people know. Why not try the flipside? I challenge you to find someone who went above and beyond and let them know how much it was appreciated. Tell his or her supervisor. Write a letter to the company. Post about it. Do something positive with your energy. For the amount of time and effort you put into complaints and nasty comments, try to put something together to reward someone. Write the letter of praise and see how that makes you feel. I know I have done it, and it has made me feel good. Try it, what is the harm? None!

I left you a page here where you can jot down some ideas and ways to show up differently and stand out from the crowd.

CHAPTER 17

Stay in Your Lane - You Cannot Be Everything To Everyone

One of the things I needed to learn more than once is that you cannot be everything to everyone. When I first started practicing, if I heard someone say she had a legal matter and needed help, the first words out of my mouth were, "I could help." I knew I had a firm behind me, and we could handle it all. Divorce, criminal, real estate, trust and estates, we did it all. I just wanted to generate business, and I did not care about the details and the specifics. I quickly learned that only certain matters and certain clients would work.

I personally could handle smaller transactional matters, sports and entertainment matters, and of course, litigation. I could do all of that myself. Someone else could do the other things, so why not just take every case we could? I am sure you can see where this is heading. I took on clients that could not pay bills, did not have a good case, and who should have never been taken on as clients. I learned quickly when I had clients with AR (Accounts Receivable) and that would never be able to pay the bills, that is a problem for me, the client and the firm. Thankfully, the firm was forgiving and worked with me and these few clients. I learned a lesson, and it carried over to my own practice.

When I left firm life, I hung my own shingle and opened my firm. I practiced what I like to call "Door Law".Whatever came in the door, I took. Legal plans. Cases I did not like. Clients who did not respect my time (or me). No matter what it looked like, I took it because I needed to build my practice and earn a living. I also took on cases that I had to learn on the fly. Now, don't get me wrong, I loved to learn new areas of the law and to figure out puzzles, but it was not where I should have been.

Once I had a decent client base, I was able to get rid of some of the clients that I did not want, or I was able to say to clients, "I do not handle that area, but I can get you with another attorney who does." I was not afraid to say no and to only handle things I knew. It felt great to be able to say, "I am sorry, but I need to pass on that." That meant I made it.

Another thing to keep in mind is that when you decide that big firm life is no longer for you, as a small firm or a solo, you will need to have a great network of colleagues and support. Build relationships with a set of "Go To's" to handle areas of the law you do not practice. For example, we handle fractional general counsel work, litigation, small business transactions and sports and entertainment. When a good client needs a will, a prenuptial agreement, or immigration help, we don't mess with it. But what we can do is send the client to other small firms or solos who concentrate in that area of the law.

If a client has a family law matter, I will send the client to someone who only does family law. Why? First of all, we don't handle family law matters. Second, if the client has more business that is not family law related, the client will come back to me (and the family law attorney would not try to take the business). Third, the client will respect you more for saying you don't handle something but that you know someone who does and will take care of the client. Fourth, many jurisdictions allow for referral fees, and you can make a few dollars, take care of the clients and help another attorney make some money. If your jurisdiction does not allow for referral fees, then disregard this and skip over it. I am not telling you this applies to everyone, so do your research and know what is allowed. Full disclosure to the client is often required, so know your rules, as you don't want to get jammed up for a few dollars. Look into it and see what is permissible.

One additional point is: don't be afraid to fire clients, and don't feel like you need to keep clients. There is an old saying that applies to boats that goes, "The happiest day in a boat owner's life is the day he gets the boat and the day he sells it." Well, in law, the two big events are the day you land a big client and get the retainer fee and the day you can tell a "problem client" that he or she is fired.

The firing of a client who you do not see eye to eye with, who does not pay bills in a timely fashion, or who is more trouble than good, feels amazing. I have been the victim of keeping clients on for too long or for the wrong reasons, but when I make the decision to let a client go, wow, it feels great. Like a huge weight has been lifted and pressure has been relieved.

So don't hang on to that client for too long, and remember, you cannot be the solution for everyone!

I was trying to figure out where in the book to put this, so I might as well do it here (as it works here as well as anywhere else). It may not be the ideal place (and you will see why I used the word "ideal" in about one sentence). Nothing is ever "perfect". What is great for you may not be great for the person sitting next to you, on the other side of the phone from you, or on the other side of an email. Nothing. This goes back to the point of this chapter, that you cannot be everything to everyone (and this additional point that you cannot be perfect).

I have a challenge for you. For one day, one week, a month, or as long as you can, remove the word "perfect" from your vocabulary. Just stop using the word. I know it will not be easy, but try it. See if you can. I have more or less eliminated it from my daily usage.

Picture this, what is the perfect drink? I might say it is a Coke Zero, a Berry Celsius that is one degree warmer than being a slushy, or a hot chocolate from Dunkin' when it is colder than forty degrees outside. To you, the reader, it might not be any of those things. So perfect is different for everyone. There was a case that I used as a teaching point when I was an adjunct professor that had to do with a ski resort being sued for advertising the "Perfect Ski Slopes" and a skier getting hurt by skiing into a tree. We discussed latent defects and obvious and open defects, but that proved the point I am making here, that perfect is subjective. So, get it out of your vocabulary (use a thesaurus if you need a replacement word).

I admit, and you can go count, I used that word a few times in this book under the well-known educational exception (I made that up, but it sounded good). When you say something with conviction and like it is a proven commodity, then it will pass muster, and no one will question you. Go ahead and kick the word "perfect" to the curb. See how it goes.

CHAPTER 18

Make Sure You Love It -- Do What You Love and Make It Show

As the final chapter of the book, Chapter 18, is upon us, I think I saved the best for last. Do what you love and show up like it is your first day. This might be the 1,000th time you have argued a motion, taken a deposition, or gone to mediation, but what about the rest of the people involved? Have they done this in the past? Is this new to them? Ask yourself that.

Also, remember the passion, excitement, nerves and the other excitement or feelings you had the first time you did something. The first time you drove a car, went to a party, had a drink, argued a motion, got an order from the Court in your client's favor, or got a pet. The excitement could not be contained, and the feeling is not easy to replicate over and over.

However, if you can look back and recall how you felt, it might change how you handle things going forward. This might not apply in all instances, but if you just think about it before you do something, that is a win. Treat it like it is your first day because it is very possible that, whether it's the person you are helping or someone in the Court you are presenting to, there is someone who is experiencing it for the first time. Think about that. I know when I have had an intern with me in Court, I remind myself it is her first time in Court, so I want to make sure she gets the whole experience. Therefore, I go in and treat it like my first time in Court. I know afterwards (regardless of the outcome), I feel like I have done my job and I have showed up.

I am sitting here at the airport trying to stay awake (it is 5:20AM), and Katerine, who is working at the desk to check people in, just gave her speech telling us about the flight being full and needing to check bags. She had so much fun with this simple task and just made everyone in the area smile and play along. I told her that she rocked it and that I was writing this book and was going to include her in it. She laughed and told me I made her day. She made my morning that much better (she was not the highlight of my day, as that was getting to talk with my Dad in person one last time).

I was fortunate enough to run into Katerine again on November 1, 2023, when I was doing the same flight to Atlanta (she was just at the counter helping out), and I got her contact information so I could send her a copy of this book when it is published. She was as great this second time as the first, and she and I both shed a tear. This time, sadly, I was going to Atlanta to escort my mother back to Florida, as my Dad had passed. I was not in a good state of mind, but my encounter and interaction with her made things just a tad bit easier.

I told my Uber driver this story, and she told me that she loves driving people around and, although she has a college degree and worked as a professional (her words, not mine), she loved driving because it allowed her to do three things she loved. #1, she got to meet all types of people (some good and some bad) and talk to them. She loved talking and asking questions. #2, she got to drive her new car, as she bought it with a bonus from her "professional job," and now she gets to drive it all day, every day. #3, she had the flexibility to do what she wanted and work when she wanted. She was tired of the grind (she put in long days doing something she was not passionate about, and she now works longer days talking to people and driving the car she loved). I believe it: do what you love and make it show. Smiles (like yawns) are contagious, and if you throw some out there, you never know what might happen.

One more thing that caught my attention was that when I was flying home from Philly last night (yes, lacrosse travel), we were delayed due to a computer issue. The air traffic controller on the runway was literally dancing on the side of the plane and putting on a show. He brought passion to the job, and it made many of us laugh and not care that we were delayed. It just goes to show how passion can be seen, felt and loved.

I wish I could give you the secret to happiness and success. If anyone says he or she can, then they are full of crap, and you need to listen to your brain and your heart. All I can say is this: ask yourself - what do you love?

I know my Dad loved spending time with his family, especially his grandkids. I also know that he would tell me to stop working when it was late because it could wait until tomorrow. Now that he is no longer with us, I hear his voice in my head saying, "It can wait." I am literally asking myself, "Can it wait until tomorrow?" If the answer is yes, then guess what, it will. But my Dad would also tell me that if it cannot wait, then not only should I go do it to get it done with, but to do it right so I can move on.

I know, professionally, I love the business of law. Mediation, negotiation, getting a deal done, and all that comes with that. What part of the law could I do without? Hands down, #1 = discovery. It sucks, and whoever thought it up should be banned from law for life. It causes unneeded disputes, increased fees and costs, and attorneys to question why he or she went into this profession. What else could I do without? Confrontation. I would rather leave something on the table to get a deal done instead of fighting just to fight.

What do you love?

Make a list, check it twice, and then see what you can do so that you can do less of what you dread (or dislike) and more of what you like (or even love). Eliminate the shit, and focus on the prize!

Go get it!

Conclusion

So now what?

You bought and read this book, took notes, highlighted sections (because that is how we have been conditioned), used the doodle space, checked out the charts and now you are ready to take your new-found motivation and tackle the world. "Where do I begin?" is what I am sure you are asking yourself.

One thing is to experiment and see what works. Give it a shot because any action is better than inaction. It is better to try and fail (yes, I used the word try) than to just never get out there. You cannot learn if you do not do.

Another is to form and refine your own Board (see Chapter 14). Identify people who are worthy of being on your Board.

Get a coach or a mentor (it does not matter your experience level, age, or profession. Just find someone you can trust and bounce things off of). This person needs to be someone you like, as we discussed, as Business is Personal (Chapter 16), and someone you trust.

Practice, Practice, Practice. That is the name of the game here. See what works and keep doing it. Stop what does not work and try something different. You don't have to keep doing the same thing if you don't like it, so experiment and see things from different perspectives.

Don't sit behind your desk and be a worker bee (unless that is what you want to do... then go for it). Again, You Be You!! I found airports, airplanes, hotels and sidelines at lacrosse events to be my happy places to write this book. Find where you want to be.

Be timely, be deliberate in your actions and go get some clients. Remember, Business is Personal. Also, remember that it is not personal, so don't take the losses (there will be losses) too personally and for too long.

Show up, and I mean really show up to everything you do. I am in the middle of rewatching "Better Call Saul," and I can tell you that James Morgan "Jimmy" McGill, known by his professional lawyer name Saul Goodman, really loved what he did, and he made sure to do it really well and with passion. From the colors of his suits to his antics in the Courtroom, he brings it.

I believe that is the secret to being the best version of yourself that you can be. Passion is the key to success and happiness. I know when I really don't want to do something, but need to do it, I have problems getting started, problems getting it done, and more than likely it is not my best effort. What do I do? I ask for help. Don't be afraid of asking for help or for a push in the right direction. You will be pleasantly surprised in how people genuinely want to help.

Another character from "Better Call Saul" that needs to be discussed here is Kim Wexler. You can see through the show how she changes as a person and an attorney. You can tell she is not happy and is looking for more. She is like many of us who just want something different. She is often seen with her hair in a tight ponytail and is all business, but then we get to see the other side of her, and we know she is not happy in her current job (she takes on pro bono clients to try to feel fulfilled, and she even sweeps up glass in a parking lot because she does not really want to go to work or handle the work that is waiting for her).

I have two recommendations – (1) watch Better Call Saul (and if you have seen it already, watch it again) and (2) find out what it is that you love and what you want to avoid. Dump the stuff you don't want and pursue the things that make you happy. Life is too short to be miserable all of the time. It is not rainbows and unicorns all the time, but it should be enjoyable more often than not.

Something else that I have found VERY helpful for me is the book *Gift-Ology* by John Ruhlin (I mentioned John's name in Chapter 16). It was a great read, and I thank Scott MacGregor and Randy Ostrow for pounding it into my head day after day to go out and read the book. Well gents, I read it two times (*Atomic Habits* by James Clear was pretty great as well, and these two and Steve Nudelberg were the persuasion I needed in order to read it)!! If you are not a "reader", both of these were great on audio and an easy listen during a long drive or a daily walk. I personally read them both and then listened to them afterwards. Like Madison says, you be you and do what works best for you.

Go PPP!!! Don't just sit there, get out there and test what works and what does not. Take mental notes (or put it in a notebook). Keep track. These are all things to help you get one percent better each day (Thank You James Clear for that mindset).

If you have questions, comments, or just want to hear more, please feel free to reach out to me at jason@askjasonweiss. com. I am ready to help you be the best version of yourself that you can be.

ABOUT THE AUTHOR

Jason S. Weiss, Esq. concentrates his area of practice in commercial/business matters, sports and entertainment and business transactions. Focusing his practice as a fractional general counsel, he has extensive experience in all aspects of the law. AS a business coach who founded "Ask Jason Weiss", Jason helps attorneys in all phases of their careers navigate through the good, the bad and the ugly of the law. As a father, when Jason is not on a phone call, you can find him pacing the sidelines at his son's lacrosse games or watching his daughter perform on stage at a dance recital. He spends quality time with his wife in their garden growing wonderful herbs, fruits and vegetables.

www.ingramcontent.com/pod-product-compliance
Lightning Source LLC
Chambersburg PA
CBHW050511210326
41521CB00011B/2410